Buck Wilder's

Small Fry
FISHING GUIDE

A complete introduction to the world of fishing for small fry of all ages

by
Tim Smith
&
Mark Herrick

Alexander & Smith Publishing

Publisher's Cataloging-in-Publication Data
Author: Smith, Timothy R.
        Buck Wilder's Small Fry Fishing Guide: a complete introduction to the world of fishing for small fry of all ages/ by Timothy R. Smith, author and Mark J. Herrick, illustrator — Traverse City, Michigan:
        Alexander & Smith Publishing, © 1995
            p: 64: col. ill.; 28 cm.

        ISBN: 0-9643793-4-1
        UPC: 7-53240-79341-5

        1. Fishing – North America – Juvenile literature 2. Fishing – United States
Illustrator: Mark J. Herrick
SH445.S65   1994   1995
799.1 [J]   dc20   LCCN 94-79423

10   9   8   7   6   5   4

Hardcover Edition . Revised 2008 and 2013

Printed in China

Alexander and Smith Publishing

A Buck Wilder Publication

Traverse City, Michigan

www.buckwilder.com

Printed by Everbest Printing Co. Ltd., Guangdong, China
June, 2013
113437

Hi! I'm BUCK WILDER
AND
I LOVE TO CATCH FISH!

This book is my guide for you. It will help all you small fry (young or old) to learn more about fishing, to catch more fish, and to have a bunch of fun. I'm giving you my best information – everything you need to know to catch the most commonly sought after fish in North America.

I know you are really going to enjoy this book – and fishing too!

Thanks,

Buck Wilder

BEFORE WE GET STARTED

Let me explain what this book has in it ...

1<u>ST</u> of all, this is meant to be a fishing guide, presented in a fun, whimsical, yet knowledgeable manner. It contains my descriptions of the most commonly sought after game fish in North America. I'll also give you important information about how to catch them, where they live, and the best bait or lure to use.

Have fun with it!

THANK YOU PAGE

Many thanks to my two best friends, Tim Smith and Mark Herrick, for all their help in writing this book with me. They are a couple of great guys – good fishermen, too – and I couldn't have done it without them. They deserve all the credit and recognition.

Have fun fishing,

Buck Wilder

CONTENTS

SECTION 1   PAGE #

SECTION 2

SECTION 3

HERE ARE THE BASICS
YOU NEED TO GO FISHING

. . . . fishing pole

. . . . good line

. . . . hooks

. . . . sinker

. . . . bait

Everything else is extra!

EXTRA STUFF

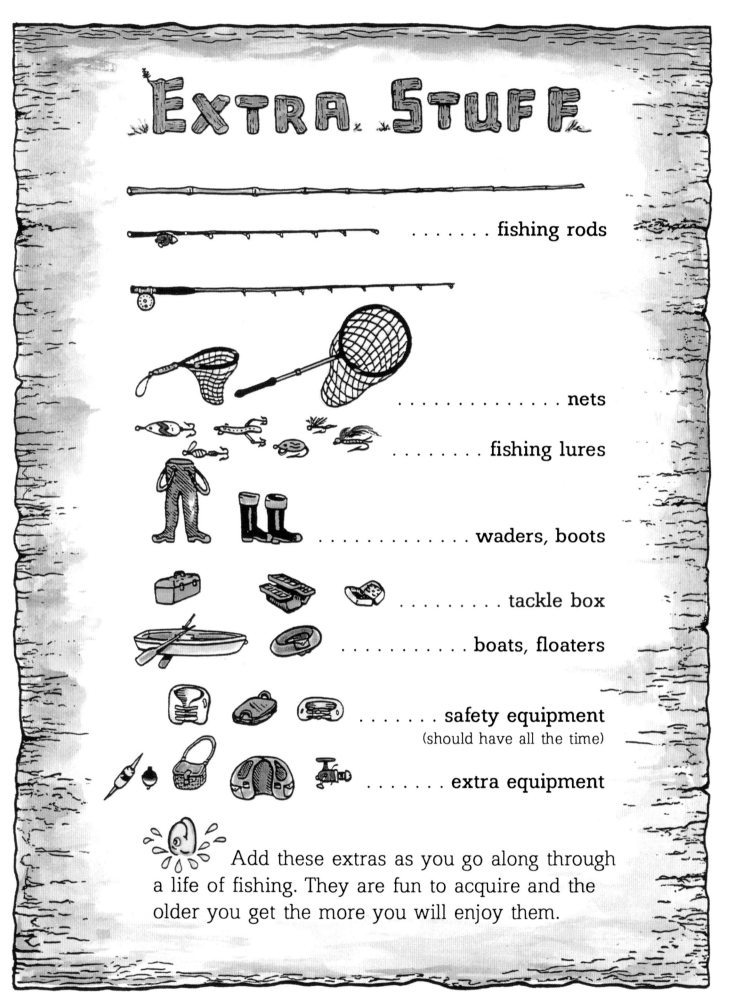

. . . . fishing rods

. . . . nets

. . . . fishing lures

. . . . waders, boots

. . . . tackle box

. . . . boats, floaters

. . . . safety equipment
(should have all the time)

. . . . extra equipment

Add these extras as you go along through a life of fishing. They are fun to acquire and the older you get the more you will enjoy them.

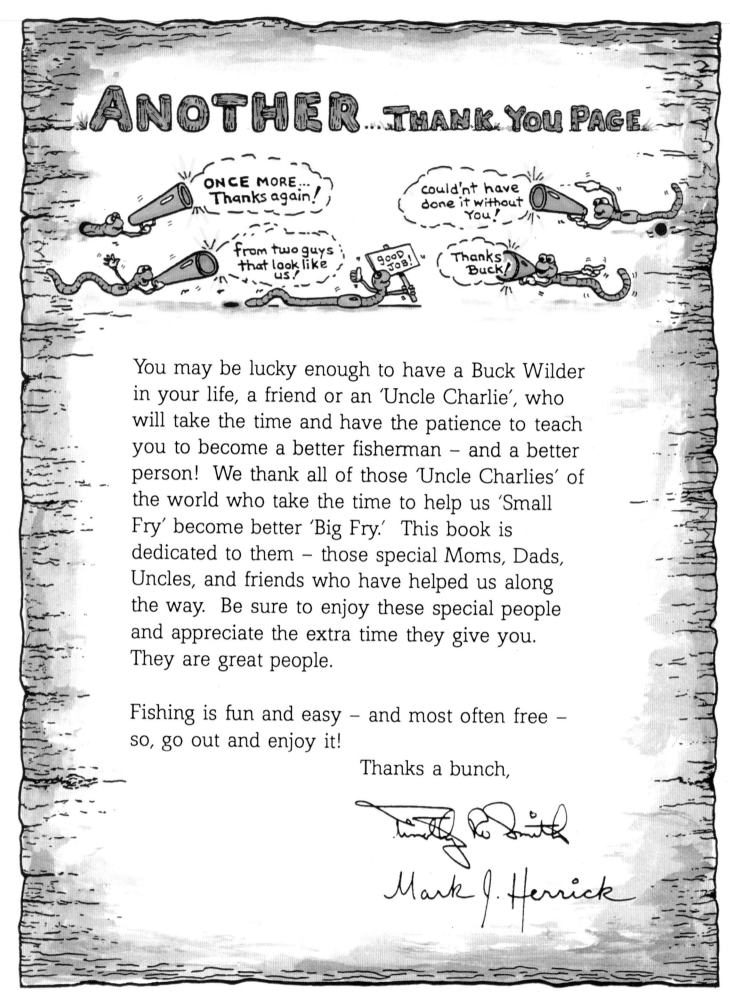

ANOTHER... THANK YOU PAGE

ONCE MORE... Thanks again!

could'nt have done it without you!

from two guys that look like us!

good JOB!

Thanks Buck!

You may be lucky enough to have a Buck Wilder in your life, a friend or an 'Uncle Charlie', who will take the time and have the patience to teach you to become a better fisherman – and a better person! We thank all of those 'Uncle Charlies' of the world who take the time to help us 'Small Fry' become better 'Big Fry.' This book is dedicated to them – those special Moms, Dads, Uncles, and friends who have helped us along the way. Be sure to enjoy these special people and appreciate the extra time they give you. They are great people.

Fishing is fun and easy – and most often free – so, go out and enjoy it!

Thanks a bunch,

Timothy R. Smith

Mark J. Herrick

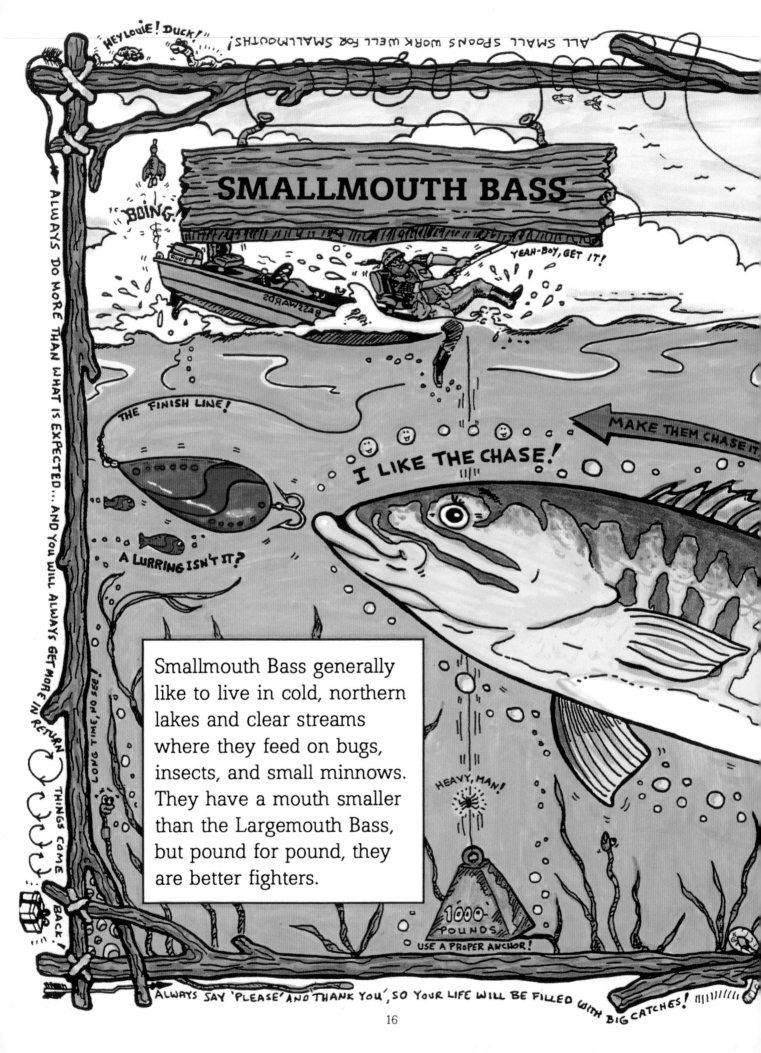

SMALLMOUTH BASS

Smallmouth Bass generally like to live in cold, northern lakes and clear streams where they feed on bugs, insects, and small minnows. They have a mouth smaller than the Largemouth Bass, but pound for pound, they are better fighters.

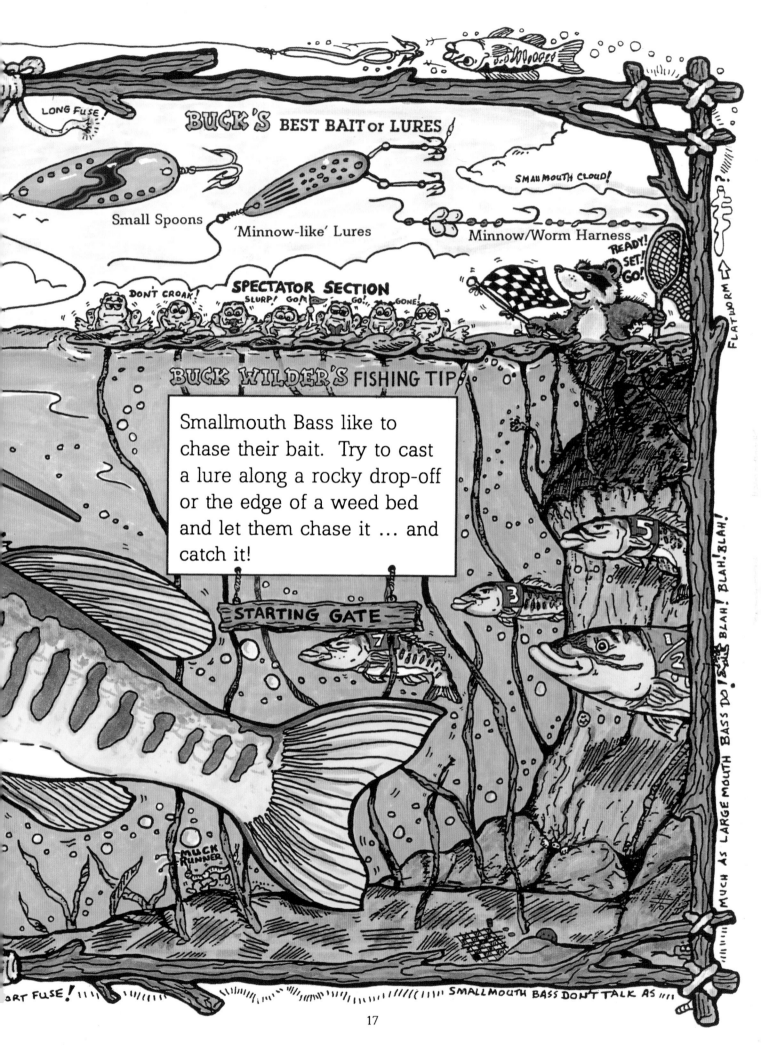

ROCK BASS

Rock Bass are common in many streams and lakes. They like to live near brush piles, weed beds, submerged logs, and of course, rock piles. They are usually smaller than other bass.

BUCK WILDER'S FISHING TIP

Fish for Rock Bass as you would for Sunfish or Bluegills. They like to 'nibble' at worms and chase little minnows. During the summer, try a 'popping bug' or an artificial fly in shallow water.

Bluegills are part of the 'panfish' family and can be found in many small to medium size lakes. They are good little fighters and a lot of fun to catch. Look for the blue on their gill.

SUNFISH

The Sunfish is sometimes called a "Pumpkin Seed" because their belly area is a bright orange-yellow with small 'seed-like' spots. You will find them in shallow lakes hanging out in deep pockets, brush piles, and drop-offs.

BUCK'S BEST BAIT or LURES

Just like most 'panfish,' the best bait is the good old worm. Put a bobber on your line, two hooks, a small sinker, and go after them!

CRAPPIE

The Crappie is closely related to the Sunfish, but it's not as pretty. Crappie are usually silvery olive with dark green spots. Sometimes called "Calico Bass", they are a good panfish to eat.

BUCK'S BEST BAIT or LURES

1. Worm
2. Small Spinner
3. Minnow

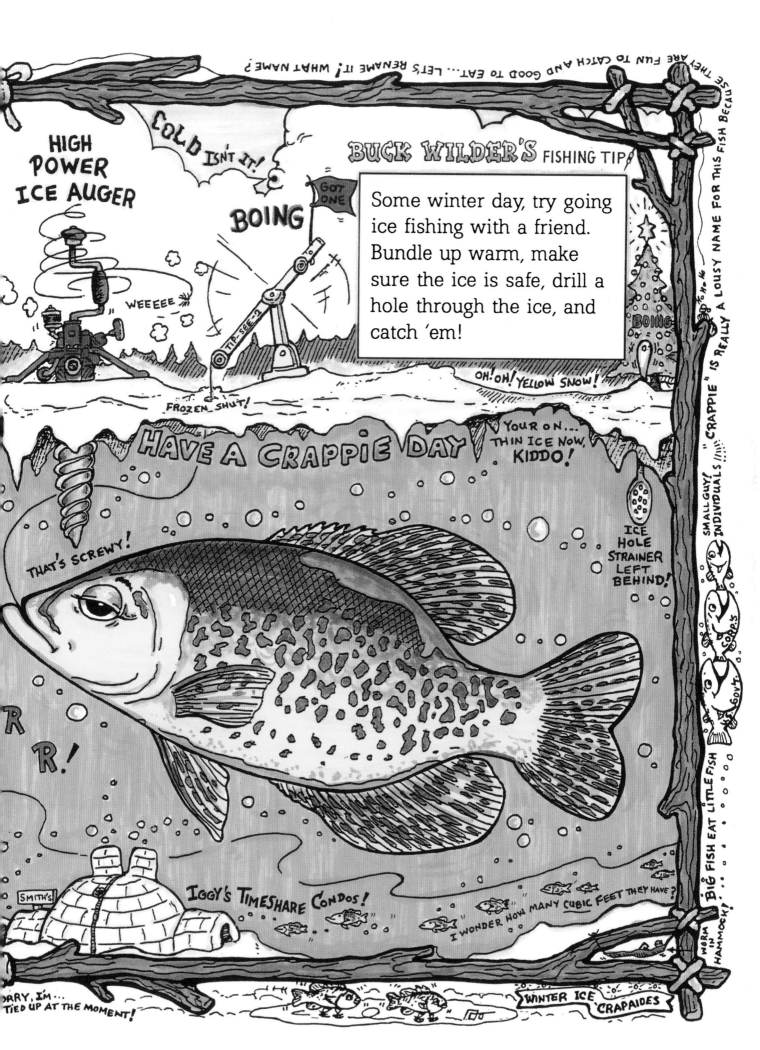

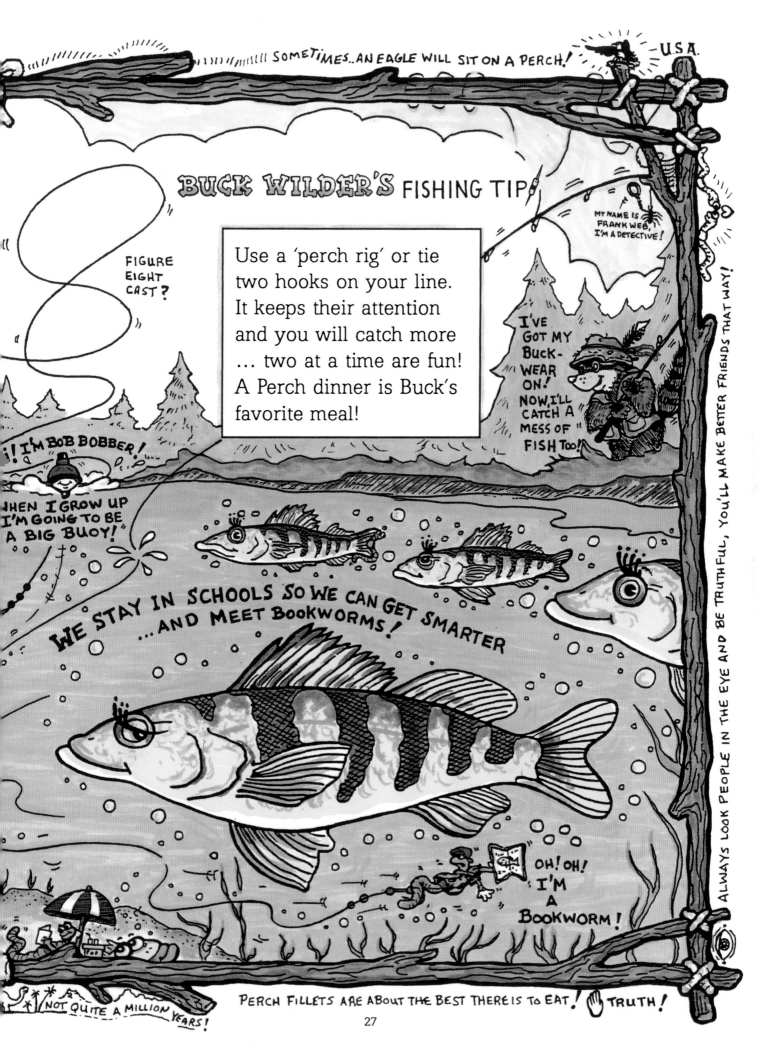

WALLEYE

Walleye like to congregate off the edges of drop-offs, mostly near the bottom. They don't like light very much, so fish for them down deep. Try the edges of weed beds also.

BUCK WILDER'S FISHING TIP

Cast a worm or small lure off the edge of a weed bed. If fishing deep, try a 'jig' with a minnow and feel for the bite on the way down! Sunrise and sunset are real good times to fish for Walleye.

NORTHERN PIKE

The Northern Pike is a very territorial and aggressive fish. They attack and eat other small fish and aquatic life. Look for them around cattails, bulrushes, and weeds ... they like to hide there.

Use mostly underwater lures, but try a surface lure too. "The bigger the lure the better" – even use those big ugly ones you find in the old tackle box.

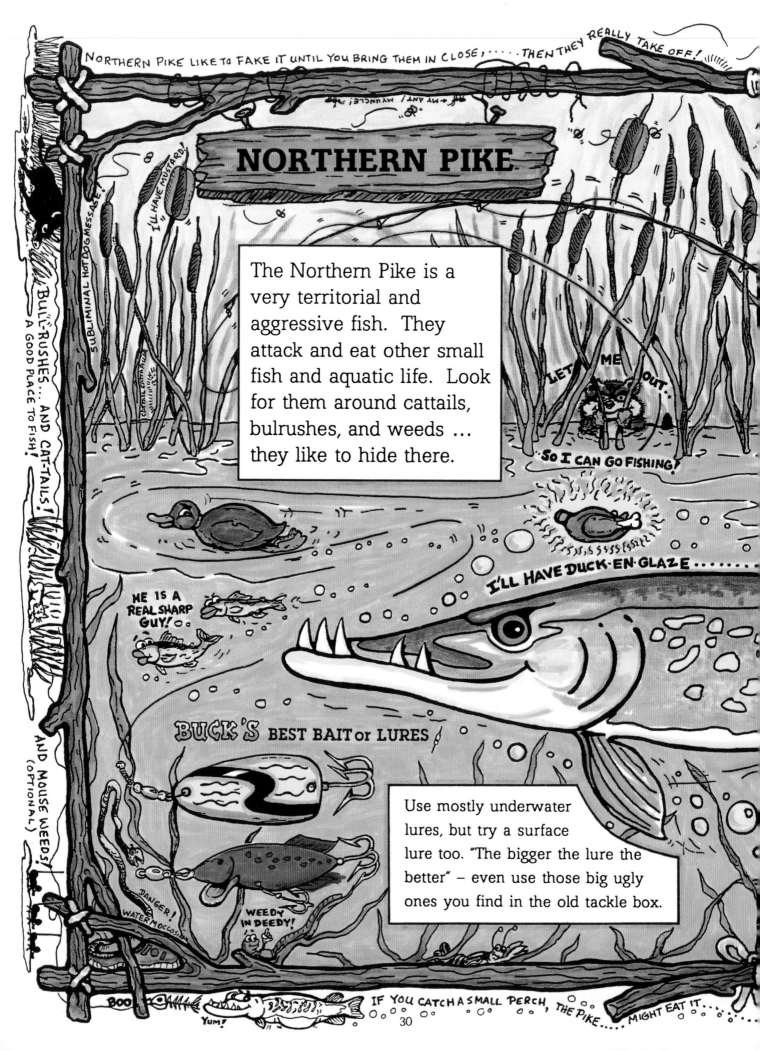

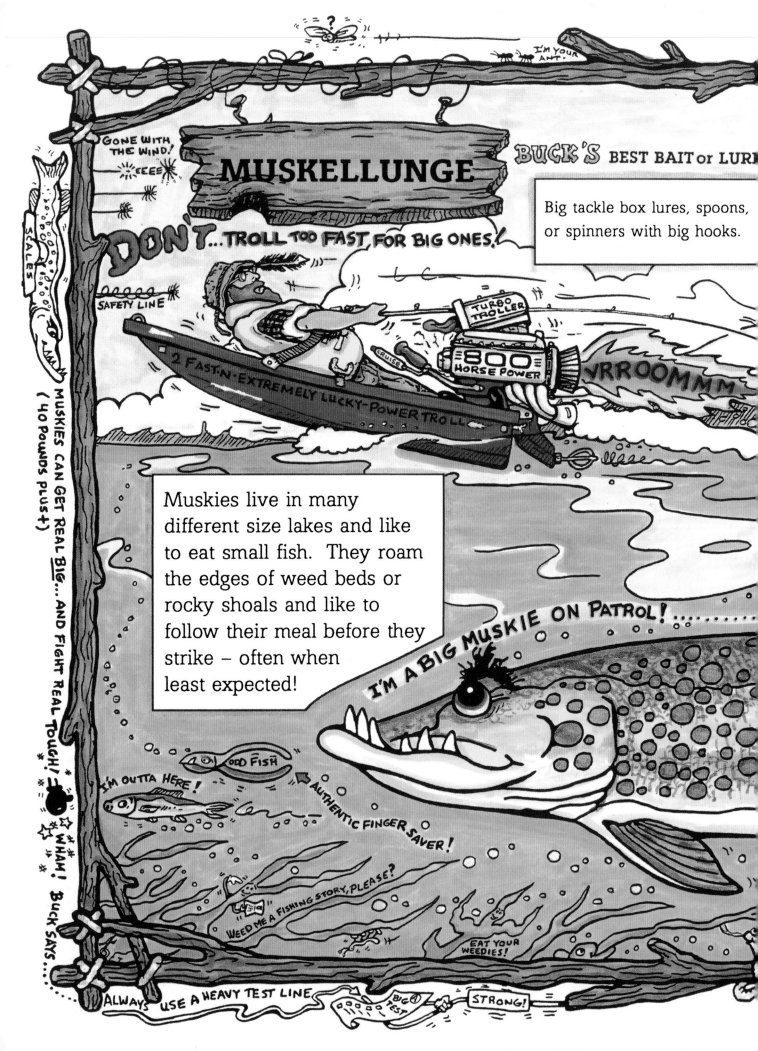

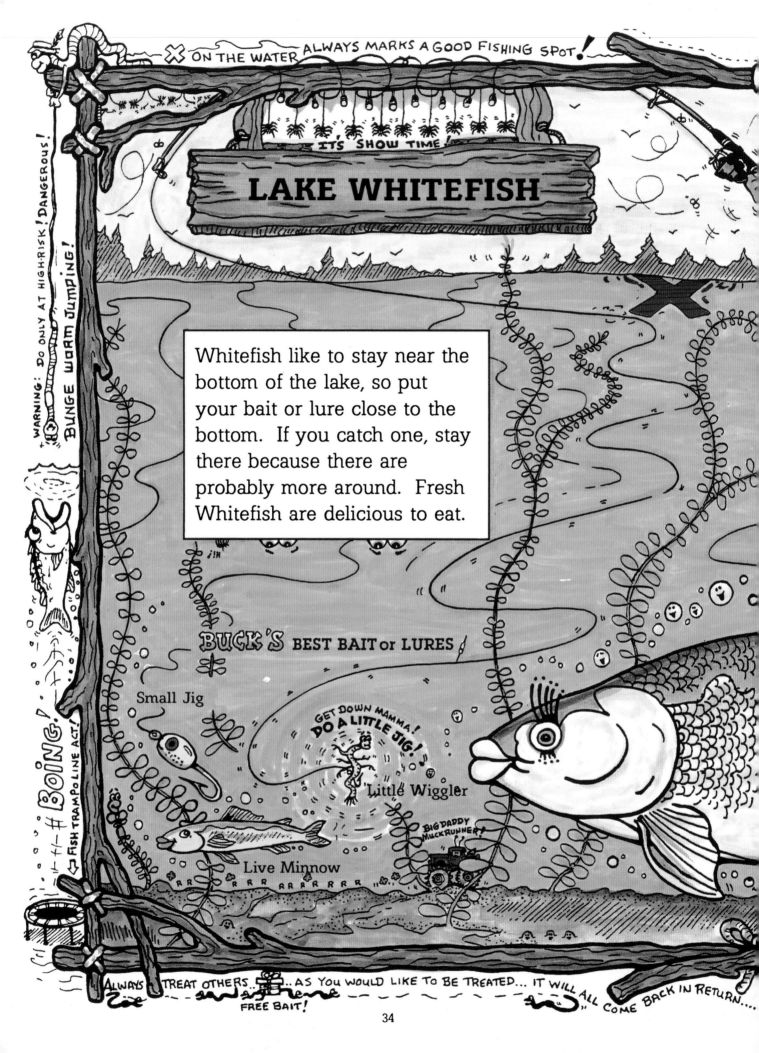

LAKE WHITEFISH

IT'S SHOW TIME!

X ON THE WATER ALWAYS MARKS A GOOD FISHING SPOT!

Whitefish like to stay near the bottom of the lake, so put your bait or lure close to the bottom. If you catch one, stay there because there are probably more around. Fresh Whitefish are delicious to eat.

BUCK'S BEST BAIT or LURES

Small Jig

GET DOWN MAMMA! DO A LITTLE JIG!

Little Wiggler

BIG DADDY MUCKRUNNER!

Live Minnow

WARNING: DO ONLY AT HIGH-RISK! DANGEROUS! BUNGE WORM JUMPING!

BOING! FISH TRAMPOLINE ACT!

ALWAYS TREAT OTHERS... AS YOU WOULD LIKE TO BE TREATED... IT WILL ALL COME BACK IN RETURN....

FREE BAIT!

34

Sometimes 'jigging' your bait will attract the Whitefish. Other times, you have to be 'real still' and feel the line softly with your finger.

Catfish have whiskers just like a cat but they don't have scales like most other fish. They tend to like the calmer water in clean rivers and lakes. Many people consider Catfish one of the most delicious fish to eat.

WHAMMMIE
BUCK WILDER'S FISHING TIP

When fishing lakes during the day, try casting around the mouth of the little streams entering the lake, or near a drop-off. At night, try fishing along the sand or gravel bars. A straight line with a bobber works about the best.

BUCK'S BEST BAIT or LURES

Artificial Fly

Spinner

WHO ME?

Worm

"or Grasshopper

In a stream you will find Rainbow Trout in the cool, fast water, hiding behind sunken logs or rocks. They are great fighters who love to jump right out of the water. Great lake/ocean Rainbows are called "Steelhead."

YOU SHOULD BE VERY QUIET!

YES TRESPASSING ALLOWED

FOR NET INCOME

IF SOMEONE ALLOWS YOU TO USE THEIR PROPERTY, GIVE THEM A FISH OR SOME KIND OF GIFT! THANKS!

BUCK WILDER'S FISHING TIP

Try the faster water for Rainbows and be ready for a real fight. Be careful and sneak up from behind very quietly!

BROWN TROUT

Brown Trout live in lakes and freshwater streams. In streams they like to hide behind logs or under the stream bank, so walk softly. They are beautiful fish and real smart too!

LAKE TROUT

Lake Trout like to live in the deepest, coldest parts of a lake, except in the springtime, when they venture into the shallower water to spawn. They are blue-grey in color with light colored spots.

BUCK WILDER'S FISHING TIP

You need a lot of line to catch these fish ... sometimes 100 feet or more. To attract their attention try trolling a 'flashy spoon' or, when fishing near the bottom, give your line a little 'jig'

SALMON

There are different types of Salmon – Coho, Chinook, Pink, Atlantic, etc. – all are very good to eat. They live in the ocean or in the Great Lakes (plus some other big lakes) and can be found in connecting rivers during the Spring and Fall of the year.

BUCK WILDER'S FISHING TIP!

Salmon are big fish, big fighters, and big jumpers. You'll need a strong line and a good, strong, fishing pole. The best way to catch one is by trolling or casting a shiny spoon or silvery lure.

FISH CHART

Largemouth Bass

Smallmouth Bass

Rock Bass

Bluegill

Sunfish

Crappie

Perch

Walleye

Northern Pike

Muskellunge

Lake Whitefish

Smelt

Catfish

Brook Trout

Rainbow Trout

Brown Trout

Lake Trout

Salmon

FISHING MADE EASY

The next few pages contain information that will make your fishing experience a lot more fun.

GIVE THIS PAGE A FLIP!

HOW TO CAST AND ...

Casting is really fairly easy ... but like anything else, if you want to be good at it, you must practice.

Pick your target and know where you want to cast. Pretend you are in front of a big clock. Point your rod at the target, bring it back to about 10 o'clock and then cast to the target, releasing the line as you cast. Let your rod stop at around the 2 or 3 o'clock mark.

PICK ME!

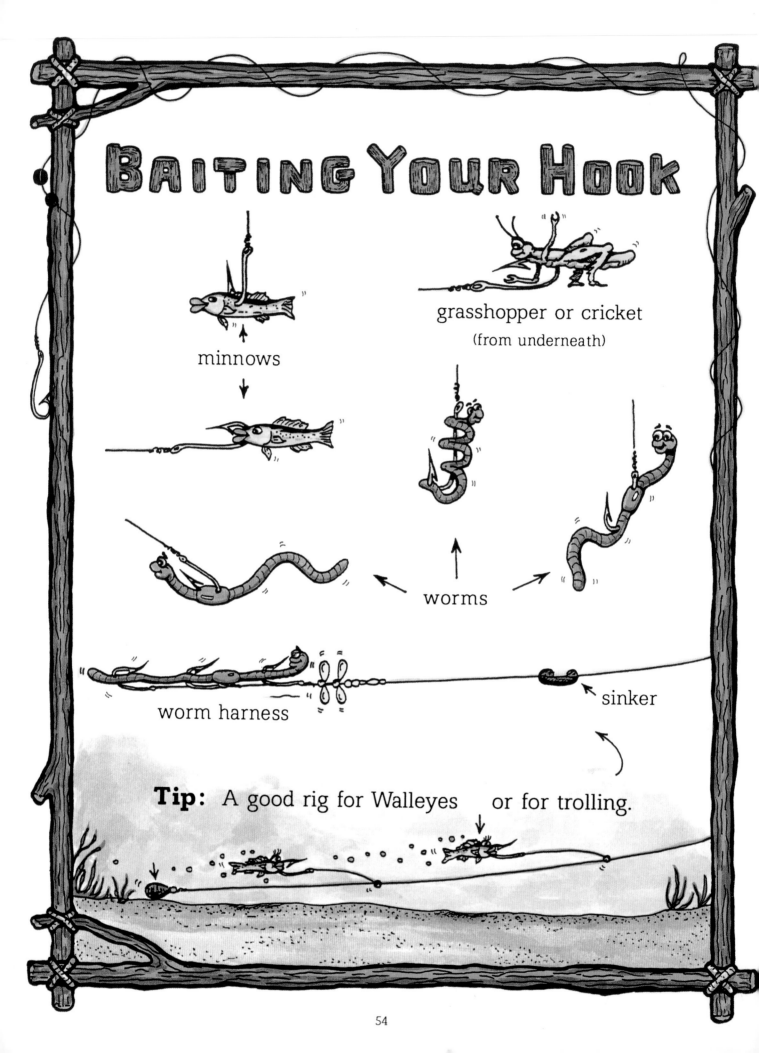

BAITING YOUR HOOK

minnows

grasshopper or cricket
(from underneath)

worms

worm harness

sinker

Tip: A good rig for Walleyes   or for trolling.

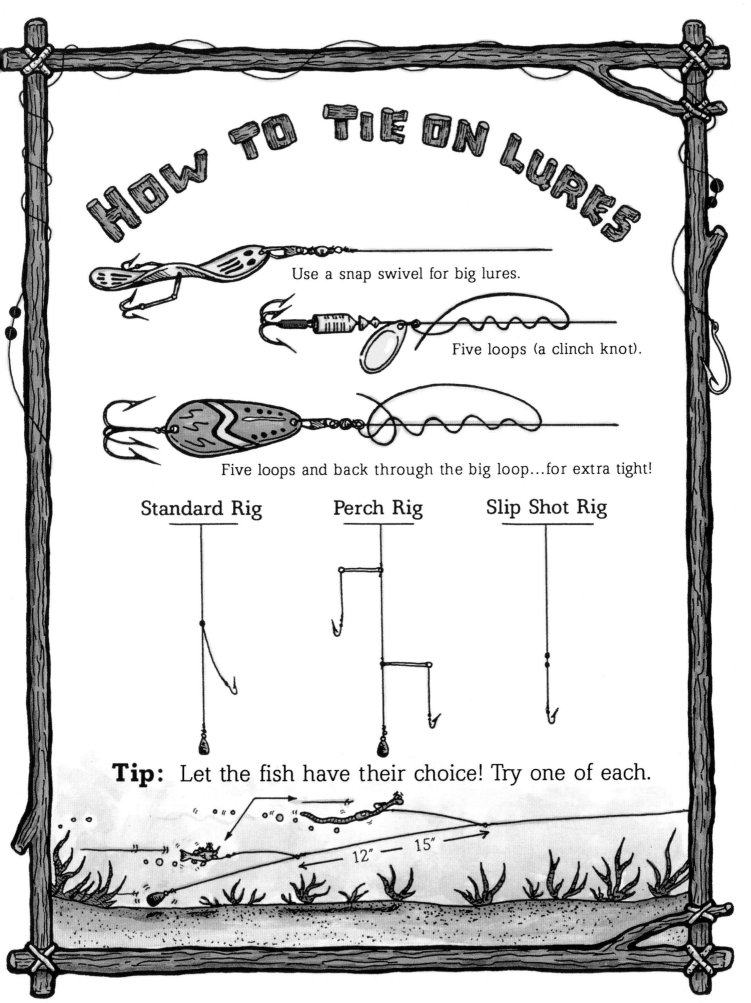

HOW TO TIE ON LURES

Use a snap swivel for big lures.

Five loops (a clinch knot).

Five loops and back through the big loop...for extra tight!

Standard Rig   **Perch Rig**   **Slip Shot Rig**

Tip: Let the fish have their choice! Try one of each.

12" — 15"

• BUCK WILDER'S • RULES TO FISH BY!

FISHING IS FUN, HEALTHY, AND GOOD FOR YOU. LIFE HAS RULES AND HERE ARE SOME THAT GO WITH FISHING!

1. GONE FISHING — I'LL BE HOME WITH DINNER! — YUP!

ALWAYS TELL SOMEONE WHERE YOU ARE GOING!

2. GAS — EVEN I WOULD'NT LIVE IN THERE!

PLAN AHEAD BEFORE YOU GO!

3.

PRIVATE — ASK PERMISSION "OR ELSE!"

NEVER TRESPASS WITHOUT PERMISSION!

4.

SPUD BAR

CHECK ICE CONDITIONS BEFORE YOU WALK OUT!

5. **ALWAYS** WEAR A SAFETY JACKET!

GET THE KIND YOU DON'T HAVE TO KEEP PUMPING UP!

AIR PUMP

BELT THOSE WADERS UP TIGHT....
....BE PREPARED FOR THE UNEXPECTED!

FREE BAIT

Worms – Can be found under logs, rocks, or piles of leaves. Dig in the ground and sift through moist soil to find them.

Grasshoppers and Crickets – You have to be fast with your hands to catch these. Be quick with your hat or try using a small hand net.

Minnows – A small hand net in the shallow water works about the best, or put some bread or crackers in a minnow catcher.

BUCK'S HOPPER HOLDER

A great little container to hold grasshoppers or crickets. It's easy to build and you can make one of these yourself.

Here is How

OLD STRING

5"

9"

Window Screen

TACK ON THE STRING HANDLE

4"

3"

1¼" NAILS

¾" NAIL

HOLE 2" COVER

4"

3"

A TIN CAN TOP OR A THIN PIECE OF WOOD

WOOD

4"

STAPLE OR...

A LITTLE WOOD GLUE IN HERE HELPS

..TACK

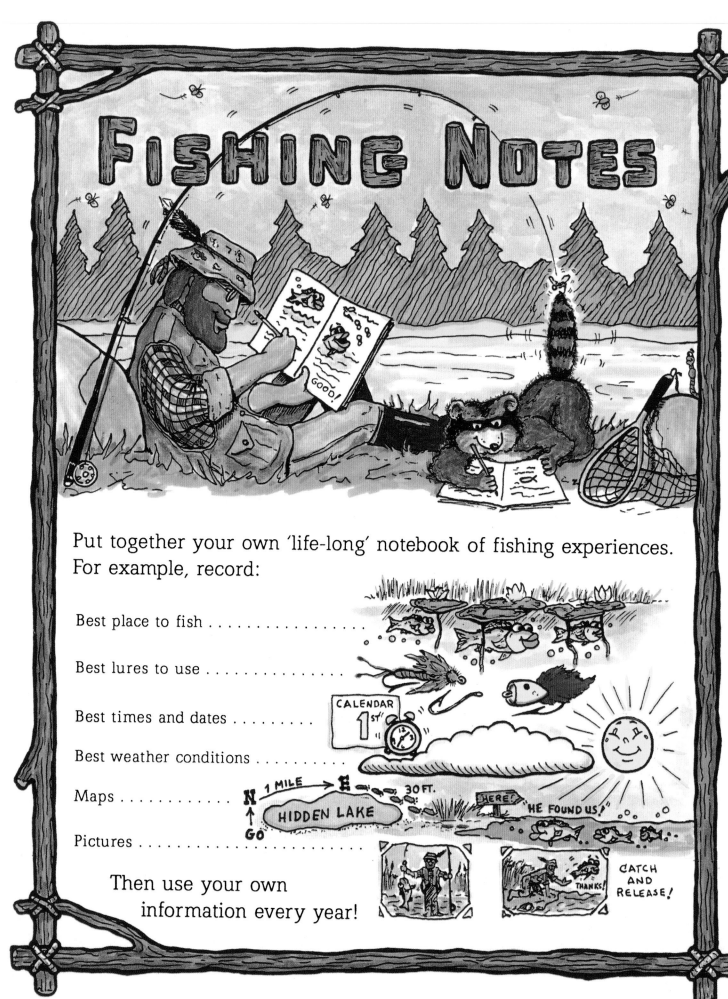

FISHING NOTES

Put together your own 'life-long' notebook of fishing experiences. For example, record:

Best place to fish . . . .

Best lures to use . . . .

Best times and dates . . . .

Best weather conditions . . . .

Maps . . . .

Pictures . . . .

Then use your own
information every year!

If you liked Buck Wilder's Small Fry Fishing Guide you will most likely also enjoy his other popular outdoor books Buck Wilder's Small Twig Hiking and Camping Guide, Buck Wilder's Little Skipper Boating Guide or Buck Wilder's Animal Wisdom book.

Buck Wilder has also written six little early reader chapter books about nature, problems that can occur in nature, and how Buck Wilder sometimes helps to solve those problems.

Most of Buck Wilder's books can be found at your local library or can be purchased from your favorite bookstore.

Hope you enjoy them!

DON'T BE CAUGHT SHORT! ORDER MORE!

INDEX

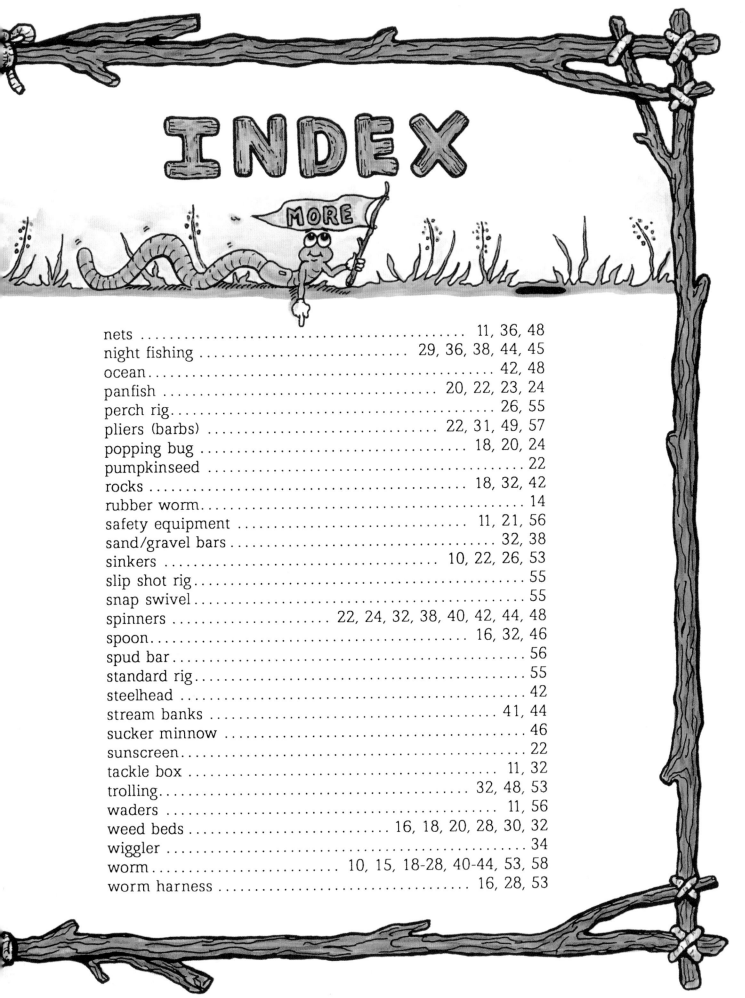

INDEX

MORE

ABOUT THE AUTHORS

"I wish I could have had this book growing up!" says Tim Smith, avid outdoorsman and fisherman extraordinaire. He lives in Northern Michigan where he fishes year round. He's so good that he even catches fish in his sleep!

"Keep this book next to your tackle box," says Mark Herrick, a life-long, professional artist who drew these amazing pictures, and has earned a bunch of Gold and Silver awards.

If you enjoyed this book and would like to purchase or see another of **Buck Wilder's** ten outdoor books just visit your local bookstore or visit us at www.buckwilder.com

Thanks!